Sophie's Ballet Dream

A tale of Courage and Self-Belief

WRITTEN AND ILLUSTRATED
BY
J.P ANTHONY WILLIAMS

DREAM WEAVER TALES

Thank You - Your <u>Free</u> Gift

Thank you for your interest in "Sophie's Ballerina Dream".

You can download your exclusive <u>FREE</u> copy of the <u>Animals Coloring Book</u> by scanning the QR code below with your phone camera

Other Books in the Series

Scan QR Code to check them out

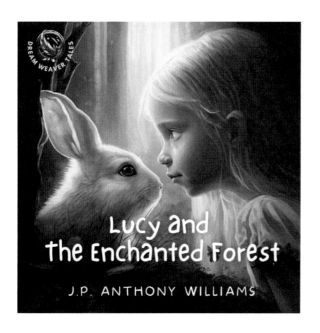

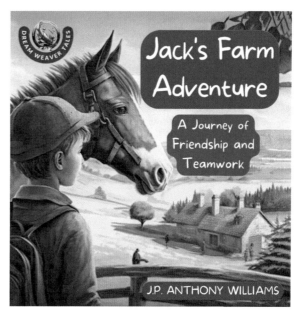

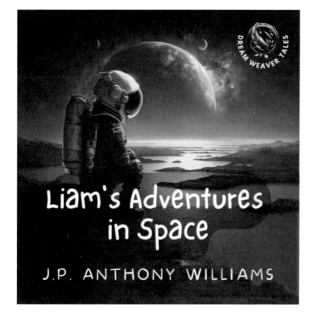

Once upon a time, there was a young girl named Sophie, who loved nothing more than to twirl around in her backyard, pretending she was a ballerina.

One day, Sophie went with her sister to see a ballet performance. The theatre was spectacular.

Sophie was amazed at the beautiful dancers and their graceful movements. From that day on, she knew that she wanted to become a true ballerina.

That night, Sophie went to bed with ballet dancing on her mind. She closed her eyes, and soon found herself inside a grand theater!

She was standing in front of a large audience, surrounded by other dancers.

They were waiting for Sophie to start a ballet performance!
But Sophie did not know what to do.

Suddenly, a colorful hummingbird that looked like a fairy appeared!

The bird held a sparkling crystal ball and offered it to Sophie with a smile.

'"Take this ball and gaze into it, Sophie," said the bird, "It holds magic that will help you become the ballerina you've always wanted to be."

Sophie was skeptical, but she took the ball from the bird and gazed into it.

To her amazement, she saw an image of herself dressed in a stunning tutu and dancing like a true ballerina!

""Sophie, you have the talent to become a great ballet dancer," the bird whispered. "Believe in yourself and all your dreams will come true."

At that moment, Sophie woke up from her dream and found herself in her bed again. With a big smile on her face, she was determined to learn ballet dancing.

She asked her parents to enroll her in ballet lessons and worked hard every day to improve her skills.

Despite facing many challenges, she remembered the hummingbird's words and continued to believe in herself.

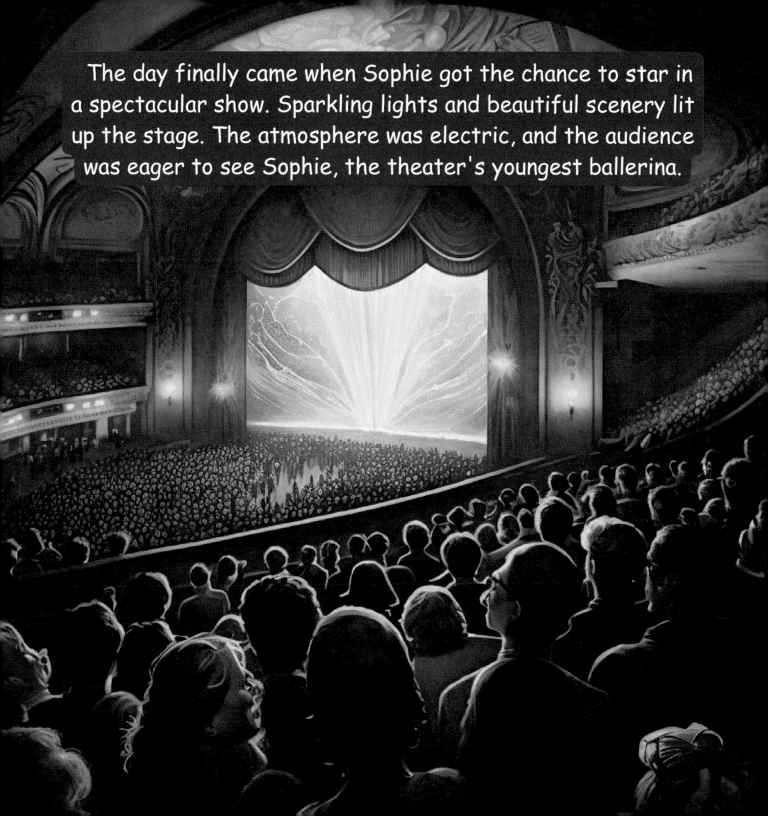

The day finally came when Sophie got the chance to star in a spectacular show. Sparkling lights and beautiful scenery lit up the stage. The atmosphere was electric, and the audience was eager to see Sophie, the theater's youngest ballerina.

As she gracefully twirled and leapt, Sophie felt a sense of pride and joy sweep over her.

The crowd cheered and clapped in amazement. They had never seen a show that was more beautiful.

As the final notes of the music faded away, the audience rose to their feet, giving her a standing ovation.
Tears of joy streamed down her cheeks as she realized she had just danced the performance of her life.

She looked out into the crowd and saw her parents, her teacher, and friends all beaming with pride.

She remembered the bird from her dream and the words:
"Believe in yourself and all your dreams will come true."
She knew that with hard work, she could one day become the
prima ballerina she desired.

Sophie had a dream so bright
Of twirling and spinning all through the night.
With grace and pace, she had no fear;
Her goal and passion for dancing was clear.

A fairy bird whispered, "Believe in you,
And all your dreams will surely come true."
With a twinkle in her eye,
Sophie took the bird's words to the sky.

After an amazing show, the crowd did stand, Applauding, cheering, and clapping their hands.
Sophie beamed with pride and pure delight,
Her hard work led to this shining night.

She became a prima ballerina,
And starred in many famous shows;
Everyone watched her with adoration;
Applauses turned into standing ovations.

Now remember, if you just believe,
You can do anything, big or small.
Trust in yourself, like Sophie did,
And you'll reach your dreams standing tall.

THE END

Thank You- <u>Free</u> Gift

Thank you for reading "Sophie's Ballerina Dream".

I hope you enjoyed it and if you have a minute to spare, I would be extremely grateful if you could post <u>a short review on my book's Amazon page.</u>

To show my gratitude, I am offering a FREE copy of the <u>Animals Coloring Book for children.</u> Download your free copy by scanning QR code below

Much Love
J.P Williams

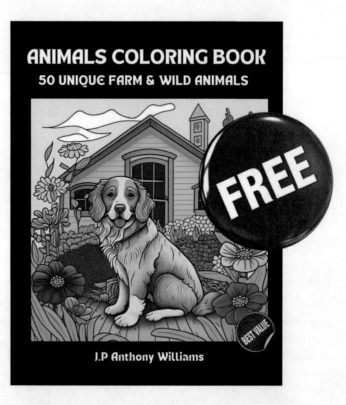

What's Next
Scan QR Code to check other books in this Series

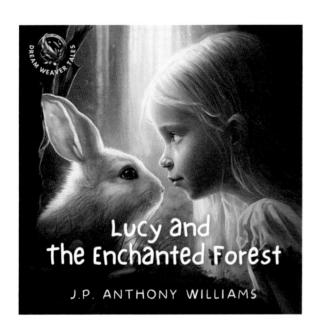

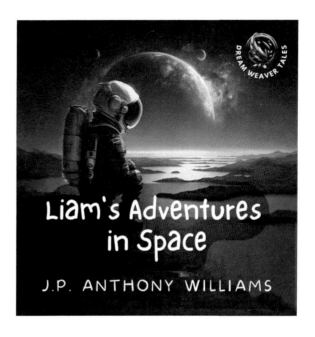

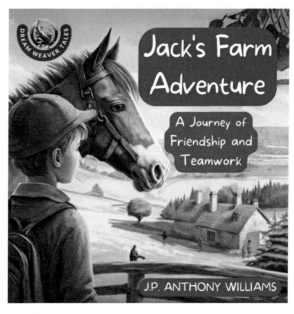

 # About the Author

J.P Anthony Williams is a bestselling children's book author, known for his enchanting tales and vivid illustrations. His stories are loved by young readers all over the world.

Born and raised in a small town, J.P developed a love of nature and storytelling at an early age. He spent his childhood exploring the woods and fields near his home, and he loved nothing more than curling up with a good book.

J.P's stories are known for their vivid imagery and richly-detailed illustrations. He takes inspiration from the natural world and from the myths and legends of his childhood, and he weaves them into tales that are both entertaining and educational.

In his free time, J.P can be found exploring new places and seeking inspiration for his next book. He is also a big advocate for environmental conservation, and often uses his platform to raise awareness about nature and its preservation.

Special thanks to my wife and kids for their support and great ideas.